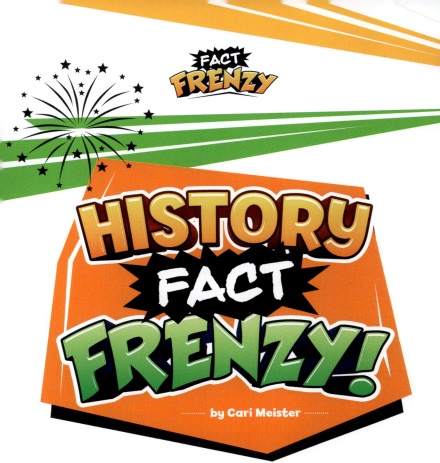

FACT FRENZY

HISTORY FACT FRENZY!

by Cari Meister

CAPSTONE PRESS
a capstone imprint

Published by Capstone Press, an imprint of Capstone
1710 Roe Crest Drive, North Mankato, Minnesota 56003
capstonepub.com

History Fact Frenzy! was originally published as *Totally Wacky Facts About Modern History*, copyright 2017 by Capstone Press.

Library of Congress Cataloging-in-Publication Data is available
on the Library of Congress website.

ISBN: 9798875233685 (hardcover)
ISBN: 9798875233630 (paperback)
ISBN: 9798875233647 (ebook PDF)

Summary: There's a HISTORY FACT FRENZY headed your way! Did you know that corncobs were once used in place of toilet paper? Or that six U.S. presidents have been named James? Dozens of bite-size historical facts are paired with fun and unexpected photos in this information-packed book. Even an aspiring young historian is sure to learn something surprising as they flip through these pages.

Editorial Credits
Editors: Alison Deering and Christianne Jones; Designer: Tracy Davies; Media Researcher: Svetlana Zhurkin; Production Specialist: Whitney Schaefer

Image Credits
Alamy: GL Archive, 34; Bridgeman Images: © Archives Charmet, 11, National Museums & Galleries of Wales, 9, Photo © The Holbarn Archive, 36; Getty Images: Archive Photos, 30, 53, bazzier, 17, Fotosearch, 44 (bottom), Goja1, 13 (top), Gratsias Adhi Hermawan, 5 (top), Hulton Archive, 8, 25 (middle), 42 (middle), 50, 57, 61, Hulton Archive/Three Lions/Lucien Aigner, 21, ilbusca, cover (bottom left), 56, Joe Scarnici, 16, Lorado, 14, mariaflaya (leech), cover, 4, 10 (bottom), Mariya Lutskovskaya (flower), cover, back cover, mikroman6, 40, 41, Photos, 38, 46, 54, Pool/Brendan Hoffman, 63, Popperfoto/Paul Popper, 32 (top), SeppFriedhuber, 49 (top), Star Tribune/Glen Stubbe, 60 (top), suteishi, 23 (middle), Topical Press Agency, 45, Vladi333, 18, Westend61, 19 (top), ZU_09, 39 (middle); NARA: U.S. Navy, 29; Shutterstock: Alliance Images, 7, AMMHPhotography, 5 (bottom), Amrit Raj (DNA), 5, 49, Annabell Gsoedl, 4 (left), 27, Artem Efimov, cover (top left), 59 (top), 64, bigjom jom, back cover, 1 (bottom), 6, Billion Photos, 31 (bottom), Brothers klia (palette and brushes), 5, 19, 46, bsd studio, 5 (top right), CkyBe (speech bubbles), cover and throughout, Claudine Van Massenhove, 62, Cold.Fire, 32 (bottom), Em Fahim, 58 (top), Eric Isselee, 43 (bottom), 55 (top and middle), evanesa, 44 (top), Everett Collection, 4 (middle), 22, 26 (middle), 31 (top), 35, 58 (bottom), evgdemidova, 15 (top), gn8 (rays and lines), cover and throughout, Gorobets (coins), cover, back cover, graham oakes, cover (top right), IQ art_Design (arrow), 18, 37, LanKS, 13 (bottom), 42 (top), lantapix (fireworks), 1, 5, 52, meunierd, 33, Michael Rosskothen, 26 (top), Ntguilty, 27 (middle), Olkita (eye), 5, 25, OMIA silhouettes, 23 (top), Peter Hermes Furian, 28, 48, Radzas2008, cover (bottom right), Rob Wilson, 47, Robert Eastman, 55 (bottom), SeDmi (leeches in a jar), cover, 4 (right), Sergiu Ungureanu (golf ball), cover, 59, SofiaV, 39 (top), Steve Travelguide, 60 (bottom), Sudowoodo, 12 (top), Tapati Rinchumrus, 12 (middle), v_kulieva (gradient background), back cover and throughout, veronchick_84 (ink bottle), 3, 37, Vital9s, 10 (top), Weiss jm, 43 (top), Yavor Nikolaev Yanev, cover (bow tie); Smithsonian Institution: National Portrait Gallery, 52 (bottom), Smithsonian American Art Museum/Gift of International Business Machines Corporation, 15 (middle); SuperStock: Glasshouse Images/Circa Images, 24, Image Asset Management/World History Archive, 20, Universal Images/Pictures from History, 51

Printed and bound in the USA. PO 6307

TABLE OF CONTENTS

A CAPTIVATING COLLECTION OF HISTORICAL FACTS

If you want to learn everything there is to know about history, you have the wrong book. If you want to learn an interesting mix of facts about history that will wow your friends and family, then you've come to the right place. The facts about leeches being used as medicine will "stick" with you forever. You might want to sit down before reading any further, because history is historically surprising.

GET READY FOR A
HISTORY FACT FRENZY!

BEAUTY, HEALTH, AND DAILY LIFE

In ancient China, small feet were considered beautiful. Parents would "bind" a daughter's feet to stunt their growth.

People used to whiten their skin with lead, which caused lead poisoning, skin damage, and hair loss.

Some Europeans would paint fake veins on their faces to make them look pale.

Throughout history, many things were used to make false teeth, including seashells, wood, rocks, bone, animal teeth, and ivory.

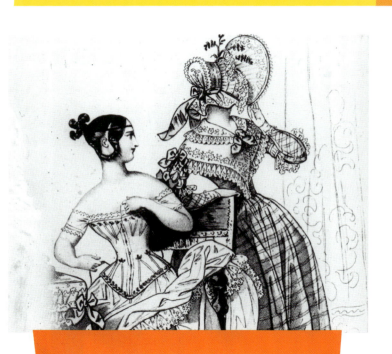

In the 1800s, whale parts were used to make corsets—fitted undergarments used to give women fashionable figures.

People in medieval Europe drank gold powder mixed with water to relieve sore muscles.

Leeches have been used in medicine for more than 3,000 years. They were put over an affected area to suck out "bad" blood.

During the 1830s in France, more than 35 million leeches were used in medicinal treatments per year.

WOW!

Once, a Parisian leech collector fell asleep and woke up to find himself completely covered in leeches.

The word "poop" was not used until around 1900.

Toilet paper was invented in China in the year 851 CE.

Other things people have used instead of toilet paper include rose petals, leaves, straw, rags, pages from catalogs or books, and corncobs.

Vikings bathed about once a week, which was way more often than most people did during that time period.

Three things most seafaring colonists had in common: head lice, big dreams, and body lice.

WOW!

The Groom of the Stool was a real job! This person was responsible for wiping a king's behind after he used the toilet.

Vikings buried their dead in boats.
They would often set them on fire
before pushing them out to sea.

A medieval feast might include
a blackbird or vulture pie.

Ancient Japanese warriors called samurai were trained in battle tactics, swordsmanship, and poetry.

FAMOUS HISTORICAL FIGURES

Famous Italian artist and inventor Leonardo Da Vinci drew plans for "floating snowshoes."

Da Vinci could draw with one hand while he wrote backward with his other hand.

WOW!

Da Vinci was a very slow painter. Many of his paintings were never finished.

Famous physicist Albert Einstein didn't start talking until he was 3 years old.

Einstein loved to sail, but
he never learned to swim.

Wolfgang Mozart, a famous composer, wrote music before he could write words.

Mozart's full name was Johannes Chrysostomus Wolfgangus Theophilus Mozart.

Mozart held a funeral for his pet bird.

Mozart wrote an entire symphony when he was only 8 years old.

Spanish artist Salvador Dalí would take his pet ocelot, Babou, out to eat.

Famous magician Harry Houdini's first performance took place when he was just 9 years old.

In his first performance, Houdini picked up pins using his eyelashes. He made 35 cents for that show.

HAMMOND·Y

DEPARTMENT OF COMMERC[E]

BUREAU OF AIR COMMERCE

In 1937, pioneer pilot Amelia Earhart and her airplane disappeared over the Pacific Ocean.

When Earhart was young, she had an imaginary Arabian horse named Saladin.

Earhart had her own aviation-inspired fashion line. It included blouses with propeller-shaped buttons.

DISASTER FACTS

A mythical triangle called the Bermuda Triangle covers more than 500,000 square miles (1,294,994 square kilometers) of ocean just off the southeastern coast of Florida.

More than 100 strange happenings have been reported in the Bermuda Triangle.

WOW!

On December 5, 1945, five United States Navy bombers vanished into thin air over the Bermuda Triangle.

The *Hindenburg* aircraft was the largest to ever fly. It was around 803 feet (245 meters) long. That's around two and a half football fields!

The *Hindenburg* exploded in 1937.
No one knows why.

The *Hindenburg* had a piano,
dining room, and smoking room.

The *Titanic*'s anchor weighed more than 15 tons (14 metric tons). Twenty horses had to pull it to the shipyard.

After the ship sank, rows of unbroken china plates rested on the ocean floor.

The last meal for the first-class passengers on the *Titanic* included 11 courses!

Violet Jessop survived three major ship crashes in her lifetime, including the *Olympic* in 1911, the *Titanic* in 1912, and the *Britannic* 1916.

WOW!

In 1898, Morgan Robertson wrote a book called *Futility* about a large "unsinkable" ship that strikes an iceberg and sinks. The ship in the book was called the *Titan*. Fourteen years later, the *Titanic* struck an iceberg and sank.

In 1820, the *Essex*, a 238-ton (216-metric-ton) whaling ship, capsized after being rammed by a whale—twice.

WOW!

The few survivors from the wreck drifted at sea in small boats for 94 days before being rescued.

Author Herman Melville's novel *Moby Dick* was inspired by the harrowing true tale.

WORLD LEADER FACTS

Queen Elizabeth I of England had more than 2,000 dresses.

In 1571, Queen Elizabeth I decreed that all men had to wear hats on Sundays.

Elizabeth I is the only English queen who never married.

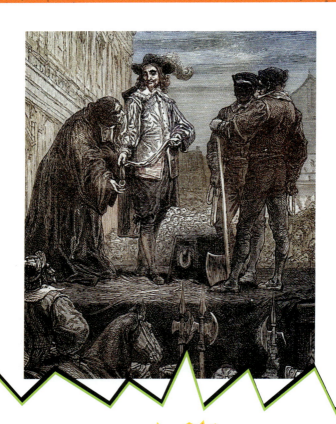

WOW!

King Charles I was beheaded for being a traitor. Out of respect for the royal family, his head was later sewn back on.

King Louis XIII of France was bald, so he started a trend of wearing big, curly wigs. The trend spread to Charles II, the king of England at the time.

In England, it is still common for judges and lawyers—called solicitors—to wear wigs.

French emperor Napoleon Bonaparte didn't like his wife Rose's name, so he changed it to Josephine.

A horde of rabbits once attacked Napoleon.

Napoleon suffered from ailurophobia. That means he was afraid of cats.

Winston Churchill, a former prime minster of Great Britain, was related to George Washington, the first U.S. president.

Churchill preferred slip-on shoes because he didn't like to waste time tying shoelaces.

WOW!

Churchill loved his bed so much that he often held important meetings in his bedroom.

Adolf Hitler, leader of Nazi Germany, was rejected from art school twice.

Hitler came up with the idea behind the Volkswagen Beetle.

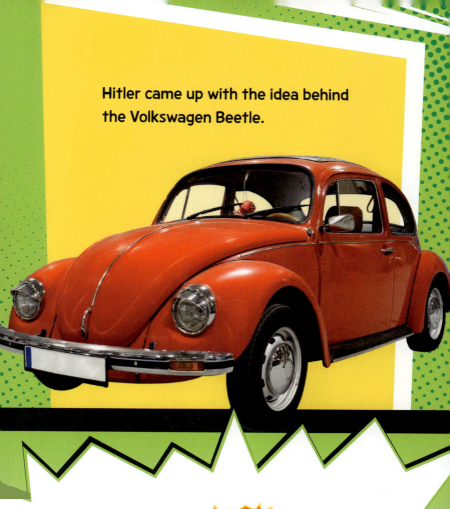

WOW!

Hitler was so worried about being poisoned that he kept "food testers" on staff.

As leader of the Mongol Empire, Genghis Khan conquered more than 12 million square miles (31 million square kilometers) of territory.

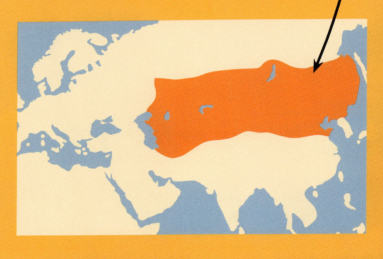

WOW!

Khan's death is a mystery, but his legacy lives on. Approximately 16 million direct descendants carry his genes.

Louis XIV was 4 years old when he became king of France.

WOW!

Sultan Ismail of Morocco (1672–1727) had more than 1,000 children.

Pu-Yi, the last emperor of China, came to power when he was 2 years old.

When her father died, Mary, Queen of Scots, became queen at 6 days old.

PRESIDENTIAL FACTS

Former U.S. presidents John Adams and Thomas Jefferson both died on July 4, 1826.

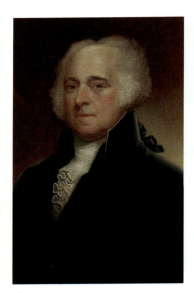

John Adams

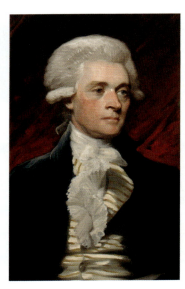

Thomas Jefferson

Despite the legend, George Washington never cut down a cherry tree.

WOW!

The "S" in Harry S. Truman does not stand for anything.

Ulysses S. Grant once got a speeding ticket for riding his horse too fast.

Calvin Coolidge had a large collection of pets, including a pygmy hippo, a bobcat, two lion cubs, an antelope, and a wallaby.

WOW!

Andrew Jackson loved his parrot so much that it was invited to his funeral. The bird had to be removed because she kept swearing.

Abraham Lincoln was a licensed bartender.

Gerald Ford worked part-time as a fashion model while he was in law school.

Ronald Reagan was a famous movie star before becoming president.

WOW!

Herbert Hoover's first job was picking bugs off of potato plants.

During the Revolutionary War, George Washington called a ceasefire to return his enemy's lost dog.

In 1902, Theodore "Teddy" Roosevelt spared the life of a bear while hunting. A toymaker heard about the story and created the teddy bear in honor of the president.

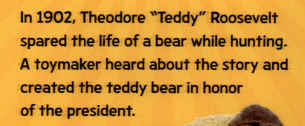

WOW!

Woodrow Wilson painted his golf balls black so he could play in the snow.

George Washington's dentures were not made of wood. They were made from a combination of hippo ivory and horse, human, and donkey teeth.

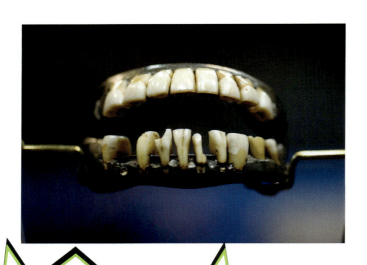

WOW!

Former president Coolidge often had people rub Vaseline on his head while he ate breakfast in bed.

Jimmy Carter was the first president
to use a nickname when he was
sworn into office.

Six U.S. presidents have had the first name
James: James Madison, James Monroe, James
Polk, James Buchanan, James Garfield, and
James "Jimmy" Carter.

James Garfield was the first left-handed president. There have been seven more since, including Herbert Hoover, Harry S. Truman, Gerald Ford, Ronald Reagan, George H.W. Bush, Bill Clinton, and Barack Obama.

BOOKS IN THIS SERIES

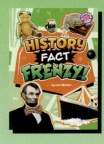